Echoes of Me: A Journey Through Silence

By L. D. Bailey

Content Warning

This collection contains strong and unfiltered
language, as well as erotic and suggestive imagery.
Many of the poems also explore sensitive themes
including grief, loss, trauma, abuse, depression,
and heartbreak.

These words are drawn from raw and lived
experience. Some pieces may stir emotions deeply,
while others speak to intimacy and desire with
equal intensity. Reader discretion is advised—
please care for yourself as you enter these pages.

For permissions and inquiries:

Voices Beyond Silence Press
voicesbeyondthesilence@gmail.com

Cover designed by L. D. Bailey
Interior formatting by L. D. Bailey

First Edition: 2025
ISBN: 979-8-218-67899-9

This book is a work of creative nonfiction and poetry. Some names and identifying details have been changed to protect privacy. The views expressed are those of the author.

Printed in the United States of America

Content Note: *This collection contains adult language, erotic/suggestive imagery, and sensitive themes of grief, trauma, and loss.*

"These pages weren't just written—they were bled into.They are stitched with silence, scarred with truth, and still sing."

L. D. Bailey

Author's Note and Dedication

My name is L. D. Bailey, and Echoes of Me: A Journey Through Silence is more than a book of poems, it's a reflection of my survival.

This collection was born from a period of unimaginable pain. I was navigating the loss of my mother, my anchor, while trying to grieve in motion. There was no pause. No stillness. Just a quiet ache and the pressure to keep going.

I was raising my children, one of whom had just suffered a serious accident, while stepping in as a mother figure to the ones my mom left behind. I was broken... and still expected to hold everyone together. I felt lost. Numb.

The poems in this book are divided into **six** series: Echoes of Her, Echoes of Darkness, Echoes of Innocence, Echoes of Silence, Echoes of Heartache, and Echoes of Longing.

Each one holds a part of my story, grief, depression, anxiety, motherhood, love, desire, and the aching process of finding and remembering who I am beneath the weight of it all.

This collection is just a snippet in a living archive of my becoming, written in the spaces between heartbreak and healing.

If you've ever had to smile while quietly unraveling, if you've ever felt invisible in your own story, if grief has touched your tongue and left you speechless,I hope these pages whispered something real back to you.

This is not the end of my journey. I'm still learning how to give myself grace. Still gathering the scattered pieces of who I am beyond the pain.

This book is dedicated to my mother.
To my sisters.
To my children.
And to the child and mother within me,
both of whom are learning to rise again.

Thank you!
With love and fire,
L. D. Bailey

Table of Contents

Echoes of Her

Echoes of Her

Grief is not a moment.
It is a landscape.
And I have wandered its terrain in silence and
sorrow,
with only poetry as my compass.

This collection began as a whisper
an ache lodged in my throat
that never quite made it into words.
But eventually, that ache demanded space.
Not just to mourn my mother,
but to grieve the pieces of myself I lost trying to
carry her.

Echoes of Her is not a tidy story.
It is not neat, nor resolved, nor easily told.
It is raw. Messy. Honest.
It is the tension between love and resentment,
between duty and desire,
between the child I was
and the woman I'm still becoming.

Each poem is a breadcrumb on the trail of my grief.

You'll meet my mother here
not just in her final breath,
but in her beauty, her flaws, her fight.
And you'll meet me
not just in mourning,

but in the fragile, defiant stirrings of my own awakening.

This is not only a tribute to the woman who gave me
life.
It is the reclamation of my own.

May you find something of yourself here
in the echoes,
in the silence,
in the space where healing begins.

For my mother, Anita.

Poems are just small pieces of our lives.
This one begins with you, "Marmee"
and the grief that taught me how to speak again.

We were often at odds, you and I.
You heard your mother in my voice,
saw yourself in my face,
and tried to rewrite your past through me.

I didn't hate you,
but I hated the weight
of being your second chance.

You were fierce, complicated,
wounded and brilliant
and I loved you.
Not blindly, but fully.

This series of poems are grace
for both of us.

A witness to the ache and the love,
and to the woman I'm becoming
now that I no longer live
for anyone else.

This is my truth.
And I carry it forward.

The Tides Within
(Three women, one body)

She was light, once
a fierce breath of wild laughter
her soul spilling colors
that left streaks
on the hearts of others
Strong
Boundless
A field in bloom
A woman wrapped
in sun-drenched hues

But the shadows came
one by one
withering the edges of her bloom
a sickness stitching itself
into her marrow
whispering tales
of hunger and sorrow

A war erupted beneath her skin
The girl she was
The addict she still was
And now
the woman told she is dying
Three versions of herself
pulling at the same thread
tangled in dusk
fighting to hold on
to what light remained

(Continued on next page)

The illness, unyielding, said
I am what's left of you now
It crept
spreading like ink
its roots winding
through bone and blood

And so she sought escape
reaching for bottles and pills
that promised release
from the chains in her chest
A crutch became a habit
A shackle
She learned to drink the darkness in
mouthfuls that drowned
out the light

She'd glimpse
the woman she'd been
a ghost caught in the reflection
Strong
Alive
A soul unbroken
But the image wavered
and blurred
fading like smoke
in the night

Death stood patient
at her door
a silent witness
to the battle within

(Continued on next page)

The girl
The addict
The dying
All of them
entwined
in the final dance

In the end
there were no sides left
Just a tired breath
a whispered goodbye
that drifted
on the edge of dawn

She left
as she'd lived
a warrior
even in surrender

Fading Light

Her breath, barely there
a hush between heartbeats.
Each day, I leaned in close
counting every rise and fall
like promises I wasn't ready to let go.

Time unraveled slowly
thread by thread
as if the world itself was holding its breath.
I traced the lines of her face
each one a story I already knew by heart.
The corners of her eyes
where her laughter used to live
soft now
like the settling of dusk.

The world grew smaller
as she grew quieter.
Colors drained from the days.
The light dimmed.
I held her hand
warm, then cooling
a tether I wasn't ready
to surrender.

The pain didn't scream
it ached

(Continued on next page)

a deep, low ache
that reached places no one sees.

I watched her fight
silent but fierce
I watched her slip
not from weakness
but because even warriors
need rest

How do you let go
of the one who gave you your name
the one who knew your storms
before you had words to explain them?
The sun rose the next day
how dare it
I still hear her
where dreams lie.

I carry her in the hush of morning
and the weight of night.
She is the echo in my laugh
the tremble in my silence
the softness in my strength.
Though her body gave in
her love did not.
She is not gone
she is sewn into me
threaded through my soul
forever.

Her Last Breath

That morning, I woke feeling off
the world pressing against my skin
a weight I couldn't name

She called to me
her voice still warm
still hers
I made her oatmeal
forced a smile
masked my unease
Because she needed me

She had an appointment
I set up her tablet
like I always did
simple, ordinary
Nothing felt urgent

She smiled
We were still okay

Then she called me again
from the bathroom
Her voice thinner this time
winded, uneven
That's when I knew
something had shifted

She was out of breath
Her body was betraying her

(Continued on next page)

I rushed to get her oxygen
tried to stay calm
Between my deep breaths
and hers
we laughed a little
soft, tired jokes
to pretend everything
wasn't cracking

I needed to be steady
She needed to feel safe

"Deep breaths," I whispered
both for her
and for me.
Then those looks

First: fear
Her wide, trembling eyes
searched mine
a silent plea
What is happening to me

Then: concern
Her gaze softened
as if suddenly worried
for me
for what I'd carry
in the moments to come

And finally: sorrow
Her soul spoke

(Continued on next page)

without words
"I'm sorry"
"I love you,
But I can't stay"

Each look
a lifetime
compressed into seconds

And then she began to fall back
slowly, gracefully
as if the world itself
had tilted just for her

Her gasps shattered the air

"Mom"
I called, again and again
a plea
a prayer
a denial
of what I was witnessing

"Mom, I'm here.
Stay with me"

Her eyes rolled back
Her body moved
but it wasn't her anymore

The air shifted.
the life,

(Continued on next page)

the soul
the essence of my mother
slipped away
in a moment
too cruel for words

I held her
watched as time fractured.
As the universe
stole her last breath
right in front of me.

And in that silence
I knew.

The Day She Left

I watched her go
not with thunder
but with a breath soft as dusk

Her eyes were open
locked on mine
then they rolled back
slow
final

No words
just the echo of her breath
fading into nothing

My sons were in the other room
laughing
playing
as children do
Life in one space
death in another
and I was the thin wall between them

The room held its breath too
as if time itself refused
to move without her

I wanted to scream
but the silence was louder
than anything I could've said

(Continued on next page)

She left
and I stayed frozen
anchored to that last look
that final unspoken goodbye

No one tells you grief is quiet.
That absence has a sound,
a hollow hum that settles in your bones
and never leaves.

The world didn't flinch.
Birds sang.
Phones buzzed.
The nurse said something
faded, distant words
I don't remember.

I only remember
my mom was just here.
Then she wasn't.

The Year I Disappeared

This wasn't my first loss.

I was fourteen
the year my grandmother died—
my safe place,
my soft place,
the only one who saw me
without shrinking or turning away.

When she passed,
something in me went with her.

I learned to smile on cue,
to nod when spoken to,
to laugh like I wasn't slowly fading
beneath my own skin.

No one noticed.
I got good at being present
without being there,
good at shrinking in plain sight.

School, home—
they blurred together,
rooms I moved through
like a ghost with a heartbeat.

I stopped reaching,
stopped expecting the world
to see the girl

(Continued on next page)

who no longer knew
how to ask for help.

Reality became
a place I visited
but didn't trust.

Because when the only person
who ever made you feel real
is gone,
what's left
feels like air you can't hold.

Crowned in Silence

I was only fourteen
when the crown was set on my head.
Not gold—
but grief.

My grandmother in the hospital,
I became the glue.
Every day by her side,
feeding her, holding her hand,
sleeping in sterile rooms
that smelled of endings.

And when she passed,
I didn't cry.
I couldn't.
Everyone else had already broken,
and I was taught to be the strong one.
To pick up the pieces,
to swallow my own ache
so no one else had to see it.

That's how I learned
strength meant silence.
Strength meant carrying
what I was never meant to carry.
Strength meant being crowned
with duty I never asked for.

Then came the heavier crown.
My mother's sickness, 2024.

(Continued on next page)

Her body fading,
her breath turning fragile.
I tried to hold her together
the way I had held the family—
but no child can stop time.

When she died,
the crown sealed itself.
Heavier than before.
Unmovable.
A weight everyone applauded
and no one offered to lift.

They told me,
"You're so strong."
But strength shouldn't feel
like suffocation.
It shouldn't mean
never being allowed to collapse.

I never asked for this crown.
It was placed on me—
first by loss,
then by expectation,
until my head bowed,
not in reverence,
but under the sheer weight of surviving.

And still,
I carry it.
Not because I wanted to,
but because no one else would.

Masked Grief

I plaster a smile on my face each day,
my mask on display in the usual way—
convincing the world,
convincing myself,
that I am fine.

But grief coils quiet
at the base of my spine.

"I've got it together,"
I shout through the cracks,
but I'm a daughter still aching
for all that I lack.

I lost my anchor,
my guide,
my flame.
And they crowned me in silence,
then called me by name.

"You're strong, you can handle it,"
they kindly insist.
But strength should not feel
like breaking like this.

I'm piecing together
what was shattered and torn,
trained for storms
since the moment I was born.

(Continued on next page)

Her words echo through me:
*"I treat you like I do
because you can take the weight."*

But I'm drowning in sorrow
they'll never equate.

Why are their tears
met with grace and light
while mine burn down my face at night?

She slipped away,
and I stayed frozen—
anchored to that last look,
that final unspoken goodbye.

No one tells you grief can be quiet.
That absence has a sound—
a hollow hum that settles in your bones
and never leaves.

The world outside didn't flinch.
Birds sang.
Phones buzzed.
The nurse said something
I don't remember.

I only remember
that my mom was here.

And then—
she wasn't

Just One Moment More

I just wanted one moment more.
One more chance to hear
 her laugh echo through the house.
To see her smile—like a sunrise after a storm.
To sit beside her, share a meal, let our hands brush,
our hearts full and connected.

I wanted one moment more to tell her I love her,
loud and clear, without rushing.
To hear her call my name
like music floating in the air.
To feel her presence next to me—steady, certain, near.

Just one moment more.
To watch her dance, light spilling from her soul
like joy made visible.
To hold her hand, still warm against the cold.
To hear her whisper, *"Everything will be okay,"*
and almost believe it.

One more moment to hug her tight.
To feel her strength in mine.
To catch her gaze and see that love still lived there,
still burned bright.
To thank her—for every sacrifice,
 every mile she walked for me,
whether I noticed or not.

I begged for just one moment more.
I wept. I prayed.

(Continued on next page)

But my prayers dissolved, and her soul faded—
finally free from pain.

Still, I carry her within me,
woven into the fabric of who I am.
And every day, with a quiet ache,
I find myself wishing
for just one moment more.

Death and Loss

In the quiet of the morning light
I search for you
my heart's first sight
Echoes of laughter still hang in the air
but now they linger
heavy with care

I remember your gentle hands
the warmth of your guiding touch
The way you listened
always meant so much
Each moment we shared
was a cherished thread
now woven into sorrow
as I tread this silence instead

The world feels colder
Shadows stretch long
But in each heartbeat
your love remains strong
Though you are gone
your soul still stays
a whisper of comfort
in all of my days

I carry your lessons
your wisdom
your grace
In every new journey
I still find your trace

(Continued on next page)

Though the void is deep
and the ache is real
in love's endless echo
your heart I still feel

One Breath at a Time

Grief doesn't leave.
It loiters. It stays.
But somehow, I'm learning
to move through the haze.
Not all at once.
Not in grand leaps.
It's in the quiet
where healing sleeps.

One breath at a time.
The first inhale feels sharp, like glass,
but it's proof that I'm here—
that this too shall pass.
I exhale the ache,
let it rise into the air.
It doesn't mean forgetting.
They're still there.

One step at a time.
Even when my feet feel like stone,
I carry the weight
but I'm not alone.
Each step forward,
no matter how small,
is a testament
I'm answering the call.
To keep living.
To keep trying.
To keep going.

(Continued on next page)

One moment at a time.
A single heartbeat.
A fleeting ray.
A chance to find hope
in the cracks of the day.

It's in the laughter
that catches me by surprise,
in the tears that still sting
but cleanse my eyes.

One day at a time.
The nights are long.
The mornings unsure.
But every sunrise
is one step closer to endure.
I learn to hold joy
and sorrow in one hand—
to honor her memory
and still make my stand.

It's not a straight line,
this road I'm on.
It's a dance with the dark,
a march toward dawn.
But I'll find my rhythm,
my steady pace.
And in time,
the shadows will give me space.

One breath.
One step.

(Continued on next page)

One moment.
One day.
Grief doesn't vanish,
but it softens.

It makes way
for love to shine through,
for hope to remain,
for me to rebuild
through the loss,
through the pain.

Legacy

I used to think legacy
meant leaving behind something grand
a name in lights
a voice remembered
a story retold

But now I know it lives
in the softest things
The way I wrap my daughter in blankets
just like you did for me
The way I hum
when words won't come

It's in my laugh
the one that sounds too much like yours
And in the fight I never chose
but somehow always carry

You taught me strength
though I never knew its weight
would feel like this
And still I rise with it
rooted in your love
reshaped by my own

I'm teaching my children
that it's okay to fall apart
That love and sorrow
can sit at the same table
That tears don't mean weakness

(Continued on next page)

They mean remembering

You live in the way I listen
The way I love hard
The way I refuse to let pain
be the end of the story

You live in me
In them
In every quiet moment
I choose to keep going

This
this is my legacy
Not the crown they gave me
Not the silence I wore

But the light I carry
The softness I protect
The strength
I've made my own

Six Months Without You

Mama... if you were still here
I'd tell you how the world fell silent
the moment your breath became memory
I held your hand
as if I could anchor you here
but even love has its limits
and yours had already given all it could

I memorized the rise and fall of your chest
each inhale fighting
each exhale forgiving
You were leaving
and I was learning what it meant
to stay behind

I watched you go
For me, it was in slow motion
It wasn't like the movies
no dramatic music
no sudden beeping flatline
Just the kind of leaving
that cracked the calendar
that split my life into
before
and after

You wore your hair in two soft braids that day
like you wanted me to remember you gentle
And you smelled like baby powder
like history and comfort

(Continued on next page)

like everything I wasn't ready to lose
I swear sometimes I still smell it
when the room goes still
but I know it's just the ache
pretending to be perfume

The days that followed were war
The clocks kept ticking
the kids kept calling
the bills didn't pause for my pain
But I did
I sat in a house full of sound
and drowned in a silence
only I could hear

Weeks passed
and I kept pretending
that grief hadn't taken up residence in my bones
Told people I was managing
like survival didn't feel like chewing glass
Smiled like I wasn't collapsing inward

Because that's what you would've done, right
And that's what you taught me to do, isn't it?

Mama
some days the air is so thick
with things I never said
I forget how to breathe without guilt

It's been six months
And I still carry you

(Continued on next page)

not in stars
not in whispers from the sky
but in the weight behind my ribs
in the pause between my laughter
in the hesitation
before I let joy have its way with me

But Mama,
I've done things I think you'd be proud of
I've built pages from pain
stitched poems out of the pieces you left behind
I've held my babies like they were breakable
but loved them the way you showed me

I show up
Even when it hurts
Even when grief laces itself into my lungs
and tries to pull me under
I don't let it win

Even when missing you
feels like drowning
with a smile stitched across my face

I'm still learning how to walk with this hole in me
Still planting seeds in ground
you no longer touch
Still trying to bloom
without your hands in the soil

These are the words I say without sound
the prayers I whisper

(Continued on next page)

into dreams where you never answer
because you can't.
You're resting
And I'm still restless

I speak them anyway
Because silence
was never strong enough
to hold all the love I still carry

And I carry you, Marmee
With grace
With ache
With forever

Echoes of Darkness

Echoes of Darkness
Preface

There are places in me
the light has never touched.

This collection was born in the quiet collapse.
In the moments when my smile was a shield.
When my silence screamed louder than words ever could.

You—Depression. Anxiety—
you took root when I was too young
to understand the weight of your whispers.
You shaped the silence, carved the hollows,
taught me how to live with shadows.

Echoes of Darkness is not about overcoming.
It is not about victory or resolution.
It is about the ache that lingers,
the hollowness that follows you from room to room,
the static that settles in your bones
when the world becomes too loud,
too bright,
too much.

These poems are your portrait—
painted in pain, outlined in survival.
They are the language of my inner war,
the claw marks of anxiety,
the numb fog of depression,
the relentless whisper that says,
"You should be fine by now."

But I am not fine.
And maybe you aren't either.
And maybe that's okay.

This series does not offer answers.
It offers my truth.
The truth of what it feels like
to be both survivor and shadow.
To hold yourself together
with trembling hands
while the world pretends not to see you fall apart.

If you've ever felt unseen in your pain,
unworthy in your stillness,
or ashamed of your sadness,
these pages are for you.

I wrote this to name you.
To know you.
To finally decide
if I'm done calling you home.

You are not alone in the dark.
I've been there too.
And I wrote this
so we'd both have something to hold on to.

Sick and Tired

I am so sick of crying—
of drowning in tears that never change a thing.

I am so tired of pretending—
of wearing smiles that crack at the edges.

I am so sick of fighting—
of battles I never seem to win.

I am so tired of holding on—
when my grip has been slipping for years.

I am so sick of wishing—
of hopes that crumble like dust in my hands.

I am so tired of listening—
to words that never match the actions behind them.

I am so sick of trying—
when effort feels like screaming into the void.

I am so tired of explaining—
of watching my truths be twisted or ignored.

I am so sick of hoping—
of chasing light that flickers and fades.

I am so tired of carrying—
burdens that were never meant to be mine.

(Continued on next page)

I am so sick of dreaming—
of waking up to the same empty ache.

I am so tired of feeling—
every ache as if my heart were made of glass.
I am so sick of living—
when each breath feels heavier than the last.

I am so tired of being strong—
when all I want is permission to fall apart.

I am so sick and so tired—
I don't know which will break me first.

Where My Shadow Won't Stay

I don't feel pain.
I don't feel peace.
Just the echo of feeling
that never quite lands.
Smiles rot on my face,
unnoticed.

Laughter sounds like glass
breaking in another room.
I am the absence
where emotion used to be,
a ghost wearing skin
with no reason left to haunt.

I wake choking
on air thick as meat,
the kind that sticks to your ribs
and rots in the cracks of your teeth.
The ceiling drools condensation,
slipping cold
down the back of my neck
like a dead thing's kiss.

This room has no corners,
just swollen walls that pulse,
breathing with me
or maybe for me.
They stretch when I scream.
They shrink when I don't.

(Continued on next page)

I claw at the seams,
but the paint peels back like skin,
wet and pink and grinning.
There are no doors here,
only apologies
that curl in my throat
and die before they're born.

The floor moans beneath my feet,
soft as bruises,
and every step tastes like iron.
I bleed without breaking.
I cry without water.

I exist in the space
between panic and paralysis,
where even my shadow
refuses to stay.

Claw Marks Beneath the Skin

Anxiety leaves souvenirs.
Not bruises,
but scratches in my thoughts,
jagged fingerprints
carved into every memory.
I try to think straight,
but the path is shredded.
Every idea bleeds out
before it can speak.

It starts in the marrow.
A twitch too deep to scratch,
like static screaming
through a cracked bone radio.
My skin doesn't belong to me.
It twists.
It whispers.
It warns.

Fingernails dig half-moons into flesh
but never reach the thing inside,
the thing that paces, that gnaws,
that hums lullabies made of teeth.
I flinch at silence
and flinch harder at noise.
The air feels too loud.
My pulse, a siren
only I can hear.

I smile with my mouth

(Continued on next page)

and scream with my spine.
Everyone calls me brave.
No one sees the bite marks
just below the surface

At night, it climbs behind my eyes,
a thousand legs,
a thousand voices,
chanting every what-if
in perfect, poisonous unison.

I curl tight,
a fist of flesh around
something I cannot kill.
And still, it waits,
patient as a shadow,
etching claw marks
into the marrow of my mind.

Static in Lace

The world hums in white noise.
I can't tune in.
Can't turn it off.
Everything is blurred and too bright.
Words come slow, then all at once.
I forget what I'm saying mid-thought,
as if my brain is choking on fog.
As if my thoughts are trying to swim
through molasses and grief.

And then she comes.
Dressed in elegance.
A black lace veil over hollow eyes,
satin-gloved fingers curling around my throat
like she's greeting an old friend.

She doesn't knock.
She seeps through the cracks in my voice,
through the pause between breaths,
through the moments I pretend I'm fine.
She lingers in my reflection,
smiles with my lips,
waits in the silence after I say I'm okay.

She whispers lullabies
in the shape of razor blades,
sings me to sleep
with the rhythm of worthlessness,
her tongue slick with rot and velvet.

(Continued on next page)

I let her in.
I always let her in.

She strokes my hair
while planting seeds of silence
in the soil of my gut.
Tells me I'm safest in the dark.
Tells me I was never built for the sun.
Tells me love is just another word
for something I don't deserve.

My limbs grow heavy with her love.
My voice becomes a memory
drowned in syrup.
Even my tears
don't want to leave anymore.

The static thickens.
Fills the room.
Wraps around me like lace.
Seduces me with numbness
until I forget the shape of light.

She makes grief look beautiful,
and I wear her like perfume.

When They Met

Anxiety arrived first,
tapping at the base of my skull,
a nervous rhythm,
sharp and staccato.
He paced.
He trembled.
He whispered catastrophes
with a mouth full of glass.

Depression came slow,
dragging her dress of dust,
a black lace veil draped over hollow eyes.
She didn't knock.
She seeped through the cracks in my voice,
through the pause between breaths,
through every place I pretended I was fine.
She sang lullabies shaped like razor blades,
her voice a syrupy rot.
She told me I was safest in the dark.
Told me I was never built for the sun.
And I believed her.

They circled each other at first,
curious shadows
casting long limbs across my bones.
Then they touched.
And the world went still,
a standoff between chaos and surrender.

Now they move in tandem.

(Continued on next page)

He pulls me into the fire.
She lays me in the ash.
He shakes the foundation.
She buries it.
Together, they built a cathedral in my chest,
lit candles with my fears,
sang hymns in my own voice.

They are the ache that stays,
woven into my spine,
settled deep in the hollows of my joints.
Their weight clings like wet denim to bone,
dragging my body inward,
folding me into a version of myself
that flinches at the light
and begs the dark for mercy.

I forget what stillness feels like
without them.
And some days,
I wonder if I ever really knew.

Whispers Behind the Eyes

There's a voice behind my eyes,
and it knows me.
It speaks in "shoulds"
and "never enoughs,"
mimicking my tone
just enough to pass as truth.
It counts my failures like rosary beads,
sings me to sleep
with all the ways I've fallen short.

They speak in tongues
only I can hear—
whispers that bloom
like mold behind my teeth.
I open my mouth to cry
and find their psalms instead,
chanted doubts,
liturgies of loathing.
They've made a temple
of my quiet decay.

I used to beg for silence.
Now I beg for clarity—
a thought that belongs to me,
a breath not filtered
through their poison.

They're polite now.
They don't take turns.
They harmonize.

(Continued on next page)

Anxiety claws at the glass,
while Depression pulls the shades.

They take my shape,
wrap around my ribs,
wear my face in mirrors
and smile with my guilt
And I kneel
between their thrones,
offering pieces of myself like communion.

They tell me what to wear,
what to fear,
who to hate—
and most of the time, it's me.

I don't fight them.
I apologize instead.
Forgive me, I whisper,
for forgetting
what life felt like
before they baptized me in doubt.

I Am the Echo in the Dark

This room isn't empty.
It's full of shadows that know my name.
They whisper in the walls,
press cold against my spine.
Here, I am safe
not because it's warm,
but because the light dares not enter.

Hope knocks.
I don't answer.
I've made a home in the hush,
where nothing is asked of me
except to survive without sound.

There is no "them" now.
No intruder.
No unfamiliar voice.
What once scratched at the door
now sleeps inside my ribs,
curled quiet, patient, permanent.

The darkness no longer waits outside.
It wears me.
It breathes with me.
I don't fear the silence
I am the silence,
sharp as shattered mirrors,
hollow as a scream swallowed too long.

Hope flickers sometimes,

(Continued on next page)

a dying bulb at the edge of vision.
But I've learned
not to reach for the light.

It scorches more than it saves
when you've lived this long
wrapped in soot and forgetting.
I am not empty.

I am the echo
of everything I buried to survive.
And when I smile,
it's only muscle memory
a twitch in the dark
where I once had a face.

Maybe

Maybe I drink
because silence is too loud.
Because when the world slows down,
my thoughts don't.

Maybe I overpour
so I can underfeel.
So I can sink into something
that doesn't ask questions,
doesn't demand healing,
doesn't make me remember.

Maybe I don't want to live.
Not in a dramatic way—
just in the quiet ache
that asks me why I bother.
Why I try.
Why I stay.

Maybe I'm tired
of pretending the pieces fit.
Maybe I drink
because I don't know
how else to hold myself together
without something burning.

Maybe I want to feel good.
Not better—just good.
For a moment.
For a sip.

(Continued on next page)

For the space between buzz and blackout
where nothing hurts
and everything is soft.

Maybe I want to stop thinking.
Stop worrying.

Stop remembering the version of me
that believed in something more
than survival.

Maybe I drink
because it's cheaper than therapy
and quieter than crying.

Maybe I just want to be free.
To let my shoulders drop.
To laugh without flinching.
To feel my body float
without the weight of "what if."

Maybe I want to fly so high
the past can't reach me.
Maybe I want to feel
anything
other than what lives under my ribs
when the room goes dark.

Maybe I don't want to be saved.
Maybe I just want to be seen.
Held
without questions.

(Continued on next page)

Touched
without fixing.
Loved
without proving I'm worth it.

Maybe I drink
because when the glass is full,
so am I.
And when it's empty,
so am I.

Maybe.
Just maybe.

Already Gone

I'm tired of waking up
just to drag this body
through hours I never asked for.
The sun feels heavy.
The air tastes stale.
Every breath...
is swallowing glass—
slow,
sharp,
unavoidable.

I drink
so I can remember what it's like
to feel something warm
touch me from the inside.
I pour
until my hands stop shaking.
Until the thoughts
stop clawing at the back of my eyes.
Until the mirror...
stops looking like a crime scene.

I don't want rescue.
Don't want trembling hands
pulling me out of the only quiet
I've ever known.
The dark?
It doesn't flinch
when I come closer.

(Continued on next page)

I'm not afraid of dying.
I'm afraid of living
like... this.

Carrying this gnawing thing in my chest
that keeps asking
why I keep breathing.

I don't want love to save me.
I just want an ending
that doesn't leave me
begging for sleep.

I'm already halfway gone.

And the only mercy left...
is letting myself
finish the fall.

What They Left Me With

I carry resentment in my chest
like coals that never cool.
They left—
my grandmother, my Yogi, my mother—
one by one,
as if my name wasn't reason enough to stay.

Grief didn't come as tears.
It came as rage.
A silent scream in the marrow of my bones
that whispered, how dare you?
How dare you slip away,
leave me to sweep up the pieces,
leave me to be the glue
when I was already breaking?

I hated the quiet after,
the hollow beds,
the way everyone else said
"they're in a better place"
while I sat in the wreckage,
abandoned,
resentful,
unwilling to forgive the leaving.

Because love was supposed to fight harder.
Love was supposed to stay.
But instead, I learned that death
doesn't care how much you begged,
how tightly you clung.

(Continued on next page)

It takes.
And takes.
And leaves you with rage you can't spit out
without choking on it.

I wanted to curse them.
For leaving me with responsibility.
For leaving me with silence.
For leaving me with a crown I never asked for.
For leaving me without their hands
to hold mine when I shook.

And yet—
beneath the ash of anger,
a coal of hope still glows.
That maybe,
when my own breath falters,
when the dark finally opens its arms,
I will see them again.
And maybe then,
I will not say how dare you.
Maybe then,
I will only whisper,
it hurt, but you're here.

The Crown I Never Asked For

I never asked for this crown.
It was forged in funerals,
in the hollow spaces where my grandmother,
my Yogi, my mother
should have stood.

It is heavy with absence,
set with jewels of sorrow,
polished by the weight of everyone else's tears
that I held when I had none left of my own.

Crowned in silence—
because no one asked if I wanted it.
Because grief doesn't wait for consent.
It presses the crown down hard,
splitting scalp,
leaving bruises no one can see.

I carried the weight,
steady as stone,
while inside I was screaming,
why me? why now? why alone?

The crown glittered for the world—
"Look how strong she is."
"Look how she carries it."
But strength was never a choice,
only the mask I wore
to keep from collapsing.

(Continued on next page)

And still, in the quiet,
when the crown digs deepest,
I wonder—
was it worth it?
Did they know what they left behind?
Did they see the cracks they carved in me?

Yet even in silence,
hope hums low,
a coal still burning under the ash.
That one day,
when breath gives way to resurrection,
when grief lifts from my shoulders like smoke,
I will lay this crown at their feet.

And finally,
I will not wear silence.
I will wear reunion.
I will wear home.

When Clouds Get to Cry

I don't like going home.
Not since she left.
Not since the world stopped
pretending it was fair.

It's been six months—
half a year of choking back air,
half a year of learning to breathe
with her absence lodged in my throat.
Half a year of pretending the earth
didn't tilt off its axis
the moment she was gone.

Everyone else
walks through the door like it's nothing.
Because I made it that way.
Because I burned myself hollow
to make it safe,
to make it warm,
to give them peace
in a space that steals it from me.

They find comfort
in the same walls that close in on me.
They don't hear the ghosts,
don't feel the weight in the silence—
because I hide it behind candles,
music,
clean floors,
and a laugh I taught myself

(Continued on next page)

to rehearse.

I tell everyone I'm okay.
Pause.
Smile like a reflex.

But it's not survival.
It's self-erasure.
It's convincing myself
that if I fake it long enough
the ache will stop clawing.
But it doesn't.

They call me strong.
Strong because I bleed in private.
Strong because I break only
where no one can see.
But the house knows.
The house rips the mask off
the second the door locks behind me.

I try to outrun it—
the echoes, the weight, the teeth.
But still, it gnaws.
The day before.
The night of.
Every damn rainy day since.

Rain falls like it's allowed to.
Like the sky has a free pass
to collapse,
to scream,

(Continued on next page)

to bleed grief across the world
without shame.

And me?
I watch from behind glass,
face pressed to the pane,
wiping my cheeks dry
before anyone can notice.

Even the heavens get permission.
Even clouds can weep without guilt.
But me—
I'm expected to carry,
to be the anchor,
to be the silence that swallows
everyone else's tears.

I am not strong.
I am cornered.
Caged by expectation.
Forced into a crown of resilience
that crushes my skull
while they call it grace.

I cry, but it feels like theft.
Like grief is a luxury
I was never meant to afford.
Because someone has to hold the world together,
and that someone is always me.

So I write.
Because paper is the only place

(Continued on next page)

I am allowed to collapse.
But paper doesn't hold me.
Poems don't fill the empty house.
Ink doesn't answer back.

And rain—
rain is the reminder.
That the sky can break,
but I can't.
Not here.
Not now.
Not ever.

Echoes of Silence

Echoes of Silence
Preface

Trigger Warning:
This section contains references to childhood sexual abuse, grooming,
emotional trauma, and dissociation. Reader discretion is advised.

Silence was never empty.
It was crowded—with fear, shame, confusion, and
the desperate hope that someone might see what I
couldn't say.

This book was never meant to be written.
Not when I was six and learned what it meant to
freeze.
Not when I was twelve and learned how to shrink.
Not even when I was fifteen and dared to speak.
Because by then, silence had become a second skin—
something I wore to stay safe, to stay wanted, to stay
alive.

Echoes of Silence is what happens when that silence is
finally cracked open.
These poems are not just memories.
They are exhalations I was never allowed to breathe
The tremble in a child's throat.
The burn in a teenager's eyes.
The ache in a woman's body when her soul whispers
no but the world expects yes.

Every page is a reckoning.
A reclamation.
A promise that I will never again swallow what was meant to
be spoken.

This collection is for every version of me who survived in
silence—
and for every reader who might still be learning how to make
noise with their pain.

You are not alone.
You never were.
And you don't have to be quiet anymore.

For every version of me who survived in silence.

To the six-year-old girl
who was touched before she understood what safety meant:
I see you.
I ache for you.
And I am writing these words so you never have to be invisible
again.

To the preteen
whose body grew faster than her voice,
who endured stares, whispers, and comments
that made her want to disappear beneath her skin—
you were never the problem.
You were always more than what they saw.

To the fifteen-year-old
who finally told someone,
who found courage in the compassion of a sister
and used that moment to crack the silence open:
Thank you for your bravery.
You changed everything.

And to the woman I became—
the one who thought being in love meant saying yes
just to feel safe,
just to feel wanted.
Even when her voice said no.
Even when her soul said no.
You are not broken.
You are not to blame.

This is for you.
All of you.
The echoes you left behind
will no longer be quiet.

The Anatomy of Voice

Speak.
With the lips
let words rise like a tide
pressed against the dam of silence.
Let them tremble, then surge
soft at first,
then fierce with purpose.

The teeth
let them bite back,
gnash through gaslight and guilt,
sharpened by the years
you were told to smile instead.
Let them know
these words are no longer tame.

The tip of the tongue
let it flow.
Let truth twirl in syllables,
undeniable, articulate
a dance of defiance
in the space between breath and boldness.

The tongue, the teeth, the lips
a trinity of testimony.
You were never meant to be quiet.
You were meant to be heard
shaped by fire,
spoken with thunder,
delivered like prophecy.

(Continued on next page)

So speak.
Even if your voice shakes.
Even if your past
claws at your throat.
Let them know
your silence was survival.
But your sound
that's revolution.

The Game

I was five
maybe six
still learning the alphabet
when he taught me
how to keep secrets
with my body

He was family
blood braided into my name
a face I trusted
until trust became something
I couldn't look in the eye

His fingers were soft
not the way monsters are in stories
but soft things can still bruise
when they slip past your skin
into the place where no
is a soundless scream

It felt dirty
like something sticky
that wouldn't wash off
no matter how hard I scrubbed

And yet
my body betrayed me
numb turned to reaction
and I hated it
I hated me

(Continued on next page)

I didn't hate him
not at first
because I loved him
because love was a twisted knot
I didn't know how to untangle
from the hands that took too much

He called it a game
said I was special
said not to tell

So I stitched silence into my bones
and learned how to smile
without letting my eyes speak

But I remember
my body remembers

And now I write
because I refuse to be
the only one
holding this weight

Secrets

It didn't happen in a dark alley.
There were no strangers.
No screams.
Just family.
Just blood.
Just me—
too young to know
that love isn't supposed to hurt
or hide.

He said
"Don't tell."
And I didn't.
Because I thought
protecting him
was the same thing as protecting me.

Because he wasn't a monster.
Not in the way stories warned me.
He smiled.
He laughed.
He hugged me
before he took too much.

What he did
wasn't loud.
It was soft,
wrong in a way
I didn't know how to name.
Shame soaked my skin

(Continued on next page)

and settled deep
into the girl
who stopped speaking without ever being asked.

I carried that silence so well
it started to look like mine.
It rewrote the way I see love.

Now I flinch at kindness.
I brace for cruelty
like it's affection
in disguise.

Intimacy became a house
with no safe room.
Touch feels like both shelter
and fire.
Desire lives beside fear,
and some nights
I can't tell who's knocking.

I was taught too early
that love can come
with a quiet betrayal—
a secret tucked beneath the skin
where no one sees.

And even now,
I crave it.
The warmth.
The wanting.

(Continued on next page)

Even when I'm unsure
if what I feel is real
or just a ghost
echoing from the first time
someone I trusted
broke me
and told me
to stay quiet.

Beneath My Skin

I bloomed too early.
My curves arrived before
my heart caught up,
carving into me
like warnings.

Boys didn't ask.
They stared.
Brushed past like it was an accident,
but their eyes gave them away.
Their hands didn't slip.
They aimed.

I learned to shrink
beneath hoodies too big
and jeans that swallowed my shape
as if hiding flesh
could keep it from being seen.

It didn't.
They still looked.
Still whispered.

The man who married my mother
always noticing, always commenting.
Uninvited observations
that lingered through the room:
"Your butt is filling out."
"That shirt is too tight."
"Your chest is getting too big."

(Continued on next page)

As if I was the danger.
As if my body was a weapon
I didn't know I was wielding.

But it never felt like power.
Only shame.

The same shame I knew
when heavy hands
taught my body to react
before I understood
what it meant.

Pleasure and disgust
danced so closely
I stopped trying to tell them apart.

I hated the way I bent,
the way I curved,
the way I invited
without ever meaning to.

I never stood in a mirror
and felt beautiful.
Only exposed.
Only wrong.
Only a thing to be blamed
for the way their eyes lingered—
like it was my fault for being seen.

I learned that my body
was not my own.

(Continued on next page)

It belonged to eyes.
To comments.
To judgment.

And I wore that knowing
like a second skin
one I still try to unzip.

Fractured Voice

I was fifteen
in a clinic
where sterile walls echoed with judgment
and strangers thought they knew my truth.

The nurse—white coat, clipped voice
confidence sharpened into condescension
tilted her head and asked,
"You're fifteen and still a virgin?"
Then, without waiting,
she answered her own question.

"Girls like you lie about that.
You're just scared your parents will find out."

She wasn't asking.
She was telling me
who I was
without knowing a damn thing.

I didn't know
I still carried the weight of shame
that I flinched at kindness
because it so often came before cruelty
that I was tired of being looked at
like an invitation I never sent.

She didn't ask.
She didn't listen.
And something inside me cracked *(Continued on next page)*

not loudly
just enough to let the fury in.

Later
when I told my sister,
the weight I carried,
she didn't question
she didn't correct
she just held me
like the truth was allowed to exist
without apology.

And for the first time
my voice didn't feel broken
just bruised
and still worthy
of being heard.

Voice of Tradition

She came cloaked in calm,
a hymn on her tongue,
grief masked in grace.
Her voice,
sweet as bruised peaches,
softened the blow
she never intended to carry.

"Is it true?" she asked,
like the truth could be willed away
with enough gentleness.

I nodded.
Heavy.
Ashamed.
Still hoping someone would rage
on my behalf.

But she didn't flinch.
She didn't shake.

Instead,
she offered me inheritance.
"All the women in our family
have been—
by men we were taught to call kin.
It's almost like a tradition."

A tradition?

(Continued on next page)

That word
landed like a slap in satin gloves.
Heavy and cruel.

As if we were bound
by some blood-soaked rite,
scars passed down like recipes,
secrets sewn into heirlooms,
generation after generation.

Then she asked,
"Have you told anyone else?"

I said no.

She exhaled relief,
a hush full of secrets.
"Well, that's good," she said.
"It happened so long ago."

As if time
was some kind of eraser
that could scrub pain clean.
As if silence
was sacred.
As if survival
meant staying quiet
and pretty
and untouched by consequence.

She didn't say,
I'm sorry.

(Continued on next page)

She didn't say,
I'll protect you.

She just folded my pain
into the same cracked keepsake box
that held hers,
my mother's,
and all the women's pain before ours.

And I knew then:
this wasn't comfort.
This was containment.

This was legacy
dressed in soft hands
and smiling denial.

But something in me splintered.
Not just the silence—
the spine of a cycle
so many before me had carried
with grace,
because no one ever told them
they could put it down.

I won't be the quiet one.
I won't be the good one.
I won't be another echo
of what was done
and left buried
in the family name.

Love Distorted

I was never taught
that love could arrive
without a shadow trailing behind it.

Touch was never just touch—
it was a question,
a demand,
a transaction.

Even in love,
my body was currency.
Even in love,
my no was just
a hurdle to overcome.

I learned to smile
through discomfort,
to disconnect mid-kiss,
to float above my body
when hands pressed in
and I didn't want them to.

He'd say,
"You don't have to move."
"Don't be like that."
"You're always tired."
And every time I said,
"No, I'm sorry, I'm not in the mood,"
his hands said otherwise.
Insistent.

(Continued on next page)

Coaxing.
Uninvited.

Pleasure became a thing
I only allowed
when I was drunk
or just numb enough
to pretend I wanted it too.

Because sober, I felt dirty.
Sober, I remembered
what it meant
to be touched
without asking.

A lover's tone
could soften me
or shatter me.
The wrong pitch
could return me
to places I didn't consent
to visit.

Love became a performance
a way to keep the peace,
to prove I wasn't broken,
to stop the questions
about what was wrong with me.

But what was wrong
was the foundation.

(Continued on next page)

Love was never safe.
Intimacy was never mine.
And desire
always came dressed in confusion.

Even now,
my body asks,
"Is it okay to enjoy this?"
And I have to answer gently
remind her
she belongs to no one
but me.

Love Reclaimed

I am not her anymore
the girl who flinched at softness,
who mistook persistence for passion,
who said yes with her mouth
while her spirit whispered no.

I no longer confuse attention
with affection,
pressure with desire,
coercion with closeness.

I've unlearned the lie
that my body is a debt
I owe to anyone who claims to care.

Now, I ask myself first.
What do I want?
What do I need?
And I listen
not with fear,
but with reverence.

I've learned that real love
doesn't push past my boundaries
and call it romance.
It doesn't demand access
and call it connection.

Now, I know
pleasure is a choice,

(Continued on next page)

not a performance.
Intimacy is an invitation,
not an obligation.
And love,
the kind I deserve,
asks.

Waits.
Honors.

I haven't found that love yet
not fully.
But I believe it exists.
And while I wait,
I am building it within myself.
Learning to know my needs,
my wants,
my desires,
before handing them over
to someone else to hold.

Because I have rewritten the story.
Because I am still writing it.
And this time,
it begins with me.

Echoes of Innocence

Echoes of Innocence
Preface

Echoes of Innocence is more than a tribute to my
children—
it is a bridge between who they are
and who I once was,
before the world taught me to quiet my voice,
to fear my feelings,
to hide in the shadows of survival.

Each of my children carries a light
that reaches places in me I thought were long forgotten.
They do not just inspire me—
they awaken me.
They speak to the small, aching girl still inside me,
the one who was told to be quiet,
to be strong, to be good... even when it hurt.

They remind her that it's okay to feel everything.
To cry loudly.
To question boldly.
To laugh until her body shakes.
To be messy, magical, and full of wonder.

It's their magic.
Their imagination.
Their resilience.
Their love and compassion—
even in their worst moments,
even after the hardest days.
It's in the little joys they notice,

the tiny things they find hilarious,
that fill them with so much life.

When my daughter embraces me,
even though touch isn't easy for her,
she whispers to the child in me
that love doesn't have to follow rules to be real.

When my youngest son crawls into my lap without a word,
blanket in hand,
just because—
he teaches me that comfort needs no explanation.

When my middle child returns after the storm,
eyes full of apology,
and I ask softly, "Are you okay?"
he reminds me of the sacredness of trying again.

This collection is made of moments—
real, raw, imperfect.
Fragments of awe
that broke open the silence within me
and reminded me that innocence isn't lost.
It waits to be reclaimed.

These poems are for them.
And for me.
And for anyone who needs to remember
that there is still magic,
still softness,
still safety
in being exactly who you are.

The Girl Who Sees Beyond

She was five
when she told me about the warrior princess—
a girl who soared on a dragon
with wings like stained glass,
fighting shadow beasts
to unlock a chest
of colors
only she could see.

The dragon's name changed daily.
The princess never did.

Her stories spilled like constellations,
each word
another star I hadn't named yet.
We went on adventures
as if the world bent for us,
magic we could summon
in the quiet between laughs.

She wrote one tale for her teacher—
the one who made her feel
like stories mattered.
Like her voice
was a kind of spell.

Now she's fourteen.
Still drawing worlds I don't have names for,
still building quiet rebellion
with brushstroke and ink.

(Continued on next page)

She stitches light into corners
I didn't even know were dark.

Her imagination keeps the fire
burning in mine.

And I wonder

What happens
if the world teaches her to shrink?
To trade wonder
for what's expected?
To stop seeing
what most of us forgot
how to dream?

I pray the warrior stays.
That the dragon never lands.
That her stories never need permission.

Because she sees beyond,
and in her eyes
are realms that remind me
how to believe again.

Love Without Rules

Your arms come slowly,
hesitant, deliberate,
as though wading into water
you're not sure will hold you.

Touch isn't easy for you.
I know,
because it's never been easy for me either.
Even now,
it asks more of me
than most people understand.

For so long,
affection came in small doses,
a pat on the back,
a pat on the head,
arms outstretched in a quiet offering,
or those rare moments
when you'd simply say,
"Hug?"
or
"Can I get a hug?"
but only when you truly wanted it.

I've learned the language of your space,
how to love you in the quiet,
without asking for more
than you can give.

But every once in a while,

(Continued on next page)

you close that distance.
Your hands find my shoulders,
your cheek brushes mine,
and the air between us softens.

No words pass your lips,
but something unspoken
ripples through me,
to the small, hidden child inside,
you whisper:
Love doesn't have to follow rules to be real.

And in that moment,
you let me in
without taking too much.
I let you close
without making you stay too long.
We meet in the middle,
where our edges don't hurt,
and love is still enough.

Little Joys

For my second child

He was three
barely stringing words together
but joy?
Joy was fluent

He and his sister played in the grass,
sunlight dripping through the trees
when he saw it:
a ladybug,
red and perfect,
crawling across a leaf
like it had come just for him

His eyes lit up
wide, round, wonder-filled
A giggle leapt from his chest,
pure and unfiltered,
like it had been waiting
his whole life to be released

He reached out
slow, curious,
his fingers trembling
with the bravery of first encounters

Then, the hesitation
The tickle of tiny legs on skin
surprised him

(Continued on next page)

but he didn't pull away
He marveled instead
At the color
At the movement
At the magic
of something so small
holding so much awe

After that,
every walk became a quest
for ladybugs,
for caterpillars,
for roly-polies
curled tight in his palm
like secrets

Joy didn't need a reason.
It only needed a moment.
A flicker of life
A speck of color
A quiet invitation
to wonder

And now,
at ten,
he still searches
not always in the grass,
but in clouds that shift,
in stones with stories,
in games
where the rules bend
just enough for imagination

(Continued on next page)

to slip in

He reminds me
that joy doesn't always come loud
Sometimes,
it crawls in softly
and changes everything

The Sacredness of Trying Again

Some storms pass
and leave the sky so heavy
you forget it ever held light.

That's how it feels
when we clash—
our words sharp,
our hearts distant.

But then,
you return.

Eyes down,
voice soft,
you ask,
"Are you okay?"

It is not just a question.
It is an offering—
a bridge built from your side to mine.
It is the first stone in the path
back to each other.

I answer,
"Yes,"
and mean it,
because what you've given me
is more than apology—
it is proof that love

(Continued on next page)

isn't about never breaking.
It's about the sacredness
of trying again.

Fearless

He had just turned eight.
Still carrying the shadow
of my mother's last breath,
gone just days before,
when grief still clung to our skin
like smoke we couldn't wash off.

Then came the scream.
The spill.
The sear.
Pain blooming where no child
should ever have to feel it.
And everything blurred,
hot tea, frantic hands,
a drive that felt like forever
with sirens echoing in my chest.

The burn unit swallowed us.
White walls, masked faces,
IVs and murmured codes.
Ten days in the PICU,
where even time held its breath.

And him,
my baby,
the one who should've broken
under the weight of it all,
sat there
still.
Strong.

(Continued on next page)

Scared,
but bigger than his fear.

He didn't cry
when the nurses asked,
"Your hand or your arm?"
He didn't look to me.

He didn't plead.
He simply breathed,
deep, steady,
and chose.

No flinch.
No tremble.
Just the sharp inhale
of a boy
becoming something more.

He spoke through the pain,
told them what hurt,
where it burned,
what was numb.

But even wrapped in agony,
he chose presence
over panic,
strength
over surrender.

And in that room,
with wires and wounds

(Continued on next page)

and a mother internally unraveling,
he became
a still point
in a world collapsing.

He was fearless,

I watched him.
Not just survive,

but command the storm
with nothing but breath
and unbelievable grace.

Because fearlessness
doesn't always roar.
Sometimes
it's a whisper in the fire
that refuses to fade.

Comfort Without Explanation

You don't ask.
You don't speak.
You simply come—
small feet against the floor,
blanket trailing like a shadow.

Before I can breathe a question,
you're here—
your weight folding into my lap,
head pressing into my chest
as if you've always belonged there.

No prelude.
No performance.
Just the warmth of you
soaking into me,
steady and sure.

Your hair smells faintly of soap.
Your hands curl into my shirt.
The rhythm of your breath
slows mine
until the noise in my head
finally stills.

You never tell me why.
You never have to.

Because in these moments,
comfort needs no explanation—

(Continued on next page)

it just lives here,
between your heartbeat and mine.

Hearts Open Wide

Their emotions come
like weather
sudden, loud,
impossible to contain.

One rages with hormones
that shake her frame,
her voice sharp,
fists clenched
at a world that
misunderstands.

But if she sees hurt in your
eyes,
she'll cross the storm,
wrap her arms around you
though touch
has never been her language.

The middle one screams
until the walls tremble.
He bites, kicks,
says things
he doesn't mean,
but feels too deeply.

Later,
when calm returns,
he finds me,
small-voiced, wide-eyed

(Continued on next page)

saddened, worried
"Are you mad at me?"
as if love could be
undone
by the mess of his pain.

The youngest shuts
down.
When sorrow finds him,
he folds into silence,
heavy and still.

But if he senses it in me,
he gathers his blanket,
climbs into my lap,
and melts into my grief
without a word

They feel in full color.
They hurt
loudly,
quietly,
honestly

And still,
they come back
They offer love
in the language they
know:
a hug,
a pat on the head,
a soft question,

(Continued on next page)

a presence
quiet gifts
that say, everything

They remind me:
a heart open wide
isn't one that never
breaks
it's one
that keeps returning
after it does

Resiliency Like a Child

Give me the heart of a child
bold enough to speak truth,
even when it stings

The kind that falls hard,
scrapes skin on pavement,
then rises again,
undaunted,
as if pain is only
a brief interruption

Let me remember how to say,
"That hurt,"
without shame.
To sit in the ache
without folding into it

Teach me to leap
without needing certainty,
To say, *"I don't know,"*
and still feel whole

To build again,
even with scattered pieces.
To ask questions
without fearing the answers.
To believe in the world
not blindly, but bravely

There is grace in a child's embrace, *(Continued on next page)*

in their way of holding what's real
without needing to soften it

Every fall is an opening,
not a failure,
but a space
where truth can land
and love can grow.

I want to stand
in the warmth of that belief.
To cry when I need to,
then wipe my face
and keep going

To live honestly,
not for the performance of strength,
but with the quiet power
of returning to myself

Give me the heart
that knows how to mend
without pretending
it was never broken

Because within the spirit of a child
lives something holy—
resilience without bitterness,
tenderness without fear,
and truth that heals
instead of harms

Echoes of Heartache

Loneliness in Togetherness

Loneliness isn't always an empty room.
Sometimes, it's a crowded space
where your heart feels unseen—
a conversation where your words
dissolve before they're heard,
a touch that grazes your skin
but never reaches your soul.

It's the quiet ache of sitting beside someone,
close enough to feel their warmth,
yet too far to feel their care.
It's offering pieces of yourself—
your thoughts, your dreams—
and watching them fall into silence,
unanswered.

It's the absence of reciprocity,
the hollow echo of a bond unbalanced.
You can be wrapped in their arms
and still feel the chill of isolation,
a ghost of connection
that never quite materializes.

Loneliness in togetherness
is the cruelest kind,
because it whispers,
"You're not enough."

But let it also remind you:
the depth of your longing

(Continued on next page)

is proof of your capacity to feel—
and you deserve someone
who doesn't just share space,
but fills it with presence.

The Loop

I rehearsed
a thousand what-ifs
inside my skull,
looping them like late-night commercials
on a channel I can't turn off.

Played scenes like vinyl
all scratch, no soul
asking myself,
what did that sigh mean?
Was it just air,
or was it the weight
of everything he wasn't saying?

I dissected his texts
like sacred scripture.
"I'm just tired."
Tired of what?
Of me?
Of the love I gave too easily?
Of the space I held
when he gave me nothing to hold?

Overthinking turns silence
into a sermon,
every breath
into a damn question mark.

I made excuses,
silk-soft lies

(Continued on next page)

to cushion sharp truths.
Said he didn't mean it that way.
Said maybe I'm just being sensitive.
Said maybe love
looks different
on different people.

But love?
Love doesn't ghost.
Love doesn't avoid.
Love doesn't make you beg
for what should be given.

He never said he didn't care,
but he didn't show it either.
And tell me
how do you measure love
that never arrives
but leaves you
waiting at the door?

So I spiral.
And spiral.
And spiral.
Trying to stitch meaning
into moments
that maybe were
never whole
to begin with.

Now my mind is a maze,
and I chase myself through it

(Continued on next page)

a girl begging the past
to rewrite itself
just once.
Just once.

But it never does.

The echo I kept chasing
was just my own voice...

The Complexity of You

You were a paradox
complicatedly simple,
a puzzle that sometimes fit
into the quiet I craved.
Your calm, when it came,
was a soft landing
in a world so loud.

I appreciated the way you spoke
not always everything,
but just enough
to show me the edges of your heart.
Even your silence held
a rare softness,
a glimpse of the man
I believed you could be.

Your intelligence shone
bright and proud.
At times, cocky,
but beneath it, a sweetness,
a tenderness that made you human,
endearing in your contradictions.

I admired how deeply you cared
for those you loved,
even if your love wore
an unconventional mask.
I saw it
hidden, but real

(Continued on next page)

a quiet loyalty,
your own kind of connection.

Still, I longed for more.
To be seen.
To be chosen.
To be a priority
without question or conditions.

I didn't want to wonder
where I fit in your world.
I wanted to feel it—
clearly, loudly, unapologetically.

And yet,
in the complexity of us,
I choose to honor
what was good,
the pieces of you that shone
when the light finally found you.

Apathy vs. Empathy

Your apathy is a fortress
cold stone walls
that refuse to crumble.
A silence so loud
it drowns the words
I never stopped speaking.
You stood there, unmoved,
while I shattered myself
against your indifference.

My empathy is a river
flowing endlessly,
reaching for shores
that never existed,
carving paths through stone
even when the stone
refused to feel
the water's touch.

You didn't flinch
as I bled my heart into the cracks,
didn't blink
when I gave you
my softness, my care.
I wanted you to feel something
anything.
But your eyes were glass,
reflecting nothing
but my effort.

(Continued on next page)

Your apathy is the weight in the room,
a shadow that grows heavier
the harder I try to lift it.
How do you feel so little,
while I feel everything
all at once?

I am a forest
burning and regrowing,
every branch aching
with the burden of care.
And you?
You are the ash
that floats away,
untouched by the fire
you left behind.

Your indifference wrapped itself around me,
snuffing out my light
with its cold, careless grip.
But still—
I cared.
I cared enough for the both of us,
even as you watched me drown in it.

You called it balance,
said I loved too hard,
too deeply.
But maybe it's you
who felt too little.

Because if apathy is your refuge,

(Continued on next page)

then my empathy is my rebellion.

I will never be like you
never stone,
never glass,
never silence.
I will always care,
even when it hurts,
because that's what makes me human.

The War Between Us

My empathy reached for you
hands through darkness,
fingers aching
to pull you from the abyss.

But your apathy—
a wall, cold and unyielding,
a fortress built to keep me out.

I spoke in whispers and screams,
in every language of love I knew,
but your silence answered back
not cruel, not kind, just... nothing.

I poured myself into you,
a flood over barren earth,
desperate for even one blade of green.
But you drank it all
without a single ripple.

Your apathy mocked every effort,
as if to say,
why try
when nothing will change?

But I couldn't stop.
That's the curse of the one who cares.

You stood still,
watching me twist and bend,.

(Continued on next page)

while I broke myself
into smaller pieces
just to fit the tiny spaces you left.
And even then,
it wasn't enough

I wanted to show you
what love could feel like
soft, warm, alive.
But you only taught me
how it feels to be invisible,
to scream into the void
and hear nothing come back.

Your apathy wasn't passive
it was a weapon:
blunt, heavy,
striking without mercy.
It crushed my hope
while my empathy
screamed to keep holding on.

But here's the truth
neither of us will say:
Your apathy wasn't strength.
It was fear
wrapped in indifference.
And my empathy?
A stubborn refusal
to accept what was already broken.

Now, I stand on this battlefield

(Continued on next page)

empty, drained, defeated.
Your apathy won.
Not because it was stronger
but because I was alone,
and love
is not a one-person war.

The Weight of Two Hearts

I felt unwanted
a hollow prize on his shelf.
A girlfriend, not a partner,
just a prop to serve himself.

Unloved.
My feelings always
pushed aside.
Every plan, every moment,
bowed down to his pride.

Unappreciated
though I stayed.
Patient.
Strong.
Made excuses for chaos,
forgave what was wrong.

I told myself,
"It's not his fault.
He's never known care."
So I gave him what I needed
hoping love would grow there.

I poured from my soul,
gave him what I never received.
And what did he return?
A refusal to try.
A refusal to believe.

(Continued on next page)

I carried the weight
of two hearts in this game.
He took the glory.
I swallowed the blame.

Now?
There's nothing left
not of me,
not of us.

Just silence.
Just emptiness.
Just... dust.

Never Enough

I offered every piece of me,
like shattered glass
rearranged to look whole.
But he never noticed the cuts on my hands,
or the blood beneath my smile.

I screamed into the silence,
but the echoes came back hollow
empty,
like I was the only one
who could hear my breaking.

How can I hold love in my hands
when it slips through like water
unseen,
untouched,
unworthy of staying?

He said my worth was more than I could see.
Yet he walked away,
leaving my soul to question
what worth even means.

I am the painting no one buys,
the song skipped before the chorus,
the story they put down
before the ending.

But I burn.
Every vein, ignited with anger.

(Continued on next page)

Every nerve,
screaming at the world for answers.

Why was I too much
and still not enough?

How can I be overflowing, drowning,
and yet
still be empty?

I want my words to shatter their armor,
to pierce the hearts of the invincible.
I want them to feel the way I feel
the ache,
the longing,
the thunder that won't quiet.

I am not delicate.
I am not fragile.
I am the storm that tears down the walls,
the flame that burns
long after the fire dies.

And one day,
they will feel me.
They will know me.
They will never forget
what I leave behind.

Almost

I've loved you
in the spaces you never stepped into
in the silences you left behind.
I built you
from every almost,
every maybe,
every someday
that never stayed.

I reach for you
like the warmth of sunlight through a window
that never opens.
You're right there...
but never mine.

I carved patience into my ribs
waiting for you to see me.
I wore hope like perfume,
thinking maybe
maybe you'd notice the way I ache
when you're near
but not close.
When you speak
but never say the words I beg for.

You love in hints,
in glances,
in midnight messages
that vanish by morning.
And I keep pretending

(Continued on next page)

that fragments can feel whole
if I hold them hard enough.

But I'm tired
of kissing empty air,
of writing poems for someone
who never learns the lines.

My heart is heavy
with a hunger
for a love that doesn't flinch,
doesn't vanish,
doesn't leave me craving
just to be chosen.

Still—
I wait.
I ache.
I crave.

Because some part of me
still believes
you might show up one day
with all of you—
not just the pieces.
Not just the almost.

Uncraved

I want to be craved.
Not liked.
Not tolerated.
Not some afterthought waiting in the inbox
of someone else's convenience.

I want to be a hunger—
the kind that gnaws at you in silence,
the ache behind your teeth
when desire has no name
but still screams mine.

I want someone
to look at me like I'm sin
they're willing to burn for.
To tremble
just imagining the curve of my voice
wrapped around their name.

But it doesn't happen.
Not for me.

I am the secret
no one ever confesses.
The closed tab.
The draft never sent.
The almost beautiful thing
you keep hidden
because you don't know
how to want me out loud.

(Continued on next page)

And still
I crave being craved.
I ache to be longed for
in ways that bend time,
that turn restraint
into ruin.

But I'm always the one
doing the longing.
Always the one
who tastes the absence
like blood in my mouth.

They don't see me.
Not the way I want to be seen.
Not the way I need to be devoured.

So I bury it.
The wanting.
The heat.
The need to be
too much for someone
and still be chosen.

I bury it in poems.
In late-night scrolls.
In sighs that go unanswered.

Because the truth is
I want to be insatiable to someone.
But I'm not.
And maybe I never will be.

To the Next Man

If you come to me,
come with stillness in your chest
not to fix,
not to rescue,
just to stay.

I've known love that was loud
but never steady
hands that held me
without holding space.
I've learned to smile through silence,
to give without being asked,
to break quietly.

I'm not asking for grand gestures.
Just presence.
Just patience.
Just truth that doesn't shift
with the weather.

I need tenderness
that doesn't vanish
when things get hard
soft eyes that really see me
not just the body,
but the ache,
the fight,
the fire I carry beneath calm.

I am no longer the girl

(Continued on next page)

who tries to earn affection.
I've become the woman
who knows her worth.
And though I'm still healing,
I won't hand my heart
to someone who won't listen
when it speaks.

So if you come
come gentle,
come open,
come whole.

Bring honesty.
Bring quiet joy.
Bring arms that don't flinch
when I trust you with my truths.

I won't beg to be chosen.
I won't shrink to be kept.
But I will love deeply
faithfully
if you're the kind of man
who loves with both hands
and stays long enough
to learn the language of mine.

Echoes of Longing

Echoes of Longing
Preface

There was a time I forgot how to want.
Grief muted me. Survival silenced me.
For years, desire sat beneath duty
buried under motherhood, heartbreak,
and the slow grind of pretending
I didn't miss being touched with intention.

But this series—these poems
this is what it sounds like
when I come back to myself.
When I stop shrinking.
When I let my fire say, I'm still here.

Echoes of Longing is not just a collection of poems
it's a slow burning reawakening.
Each one is a flicker of want,
a pulse of memory,
a moan caught between breath and bravery.

These are not poems meant to make you comfortable.
They are meant to make you remember.

The ache.
The edge.
The thrill of being opened slowly.
The danger of being seen too deeply.
The power in choosing to surrender
on your terms.

This is for the women who've been told
to hush their hunger.
This is for the ones who ache out loud.

If you're here,
I hope you're ready to feel

To the woman I buried
beneath responsibility, silence, and survival
this is for you.
For your skin, your scream, your shadow.
You didn't disappear.
You were just waiting
for permission to burn again.

Longing of Hope

They handed me a box.
Not a body.
Not a goodbye.
No last kiss,
no hand to hold—
just... a box.
Ashes.
Bone dust.
A whole life,
compressed into something I could carry...
but never put down.

Grief didn't knock.
It seeped in—
through my skin,
into my breath,
into everything I touched.

It didn't scream.
It settled.
Sat heavy on my chest
and waited.

I don't visit a grave.
There isn't one.
I visit the mirror.
Because that's where she lives now.

I see her
every time the mirror finds me.
(Continued on next page)

Her face lives in mine
dulled,
like a photograph left in the rain.

A watered-down reflection
of a woman who once held the world together
with a smile that cracked under its weight
and a spine stitched from prayer.

And I?
I am what remains.

That's when depression came
sank its teeth into me,
slow at first,
like it was testing the taste.
It didn't rush.

It settled in my bones,
crept through my veins,
and stayed.
Like smoke
that forgot how to rise.

Some mornings,
I wake up angry
that I woke up at all.

But I do.
Not because I want to—
because my body keeps choosing
to stay

(Continued on next page)

And maybe...
Maybe that's all hope is.

Maybe hope doesn't come
like sunlight.
Maybe it comes like this
like ashes that refuse to scatter,
like breath
you didn't think you'd take.

Like looking in the mirror
and seeing her
in you
not as a ghost,
but as a reason
to try.

Not whole.
But here.

Still standing in the ruins.
Still daring to breathe.

And maybe...
just maybe,
that's what hope is.

Longing of Healing

They talk about healing
like it's gentle.
Like it's soft light
and slow mornings.
But no one told me
healing starts with bleeding.
With screaming into pillows,
shaking in the dark
until the storm runs out of name.

No one told me
that to heal
is to relive
everything that broke you.
Just slower this time.
Just awake this time.
Just alone.

There were days
my body didn't feel like mine
like it belonged to grief,
like it belonged to the ache.
And maybe it did.

Because I was still carrying pain
that didn't have language.
Still stitching shut wounds
I was told didn't exist.
Still learning how to be
a person

(Continued on next page)

who deserves breath
without apology.

Healing
wasn't sunlight.
It was sitting in the dark
and not rushing the dawn.

They talk about healing
like it's gentle.It was choosing
not to disappear
even when disappearing
felt like mercy.

It was brushing my own hair
with trembling hands.
Eating soup
even when I hated myself.
It was standing in the mirror
and whispering,
"Not yet...
but maybe someday."

And today?
I am not whole.
But I am here.

And maybe
maybe that's what healing looks like.
Not beautiful.
But possible.

Longing to Be Seen

Don't tell me I'm beautiful
if you only mean it
when I look like I'm not hurting.

If your eyes
can't stay with mine
when the scars show,
when the makeup fades,
when the light hits my body
and the stretch marks speak louder
than skin.

Because this body?
It's not polished.
It's not untouched.
It's a battlefield
stitched with grace.

Every line,
every dip,
every space they say shouldn't be there
is a story.
And most people don't want to hear them.
Not really.

They want beauty
without the backstory.
Desire without depth.
A woman they can stare at
but not sit with.

(Continued on next page)

But I am not here
to be stared at.
I am here
to be seen.

I've lived lifetimes
in this skin.
Carried silence in my jaw
where teeth used to sit.
Carried shame in my stomach
where softness lives now.

I've watched people look away
when I smiled too wide
or existed too loudly—
like honesty made them flinch.

But here's the truth:

I'm not asking
for your comfort.
I'm asking
for your witness.

See me
when I'm not filtered.
See me
when I'm tired
and still choosing to show up.
See me
when my body tells stories
you don't know how to hold..

(Continued on next page)

Because I am not
your before photo.
Not your cautionary tale.
Not your fix-it project
in a dress.

I am woman.
I am map.
I am miracle.

And if you cannot see me whole
scars, stretch marks, silence and all
then don't you dare call it love.

Longing of Grace

I am tired
of performing strength
for people who would drown
in a fraction of what I carry.

Tired of being applauded
for surviving what should've destroyed me,
while still being judged
for how I limp.

They want resilience
but only if it's pretty.
Only if I rise
without rage.
Only if I bleed quietly
and clean up after myself.

But I am done
being sacred only when I'm silent.

Give me grace.
Not because I earned it
in a way that makes you comfortable,
but because I damn well deserve it.

Let me cry ugly.
Let me break
without warning.
Let me feel too much
too loud,

(Continued on next page)

too often.

Don't hand me another compliment
for holding it together.
Hand me a blanket
when I can't.

Because some days,
I don't want to inspire.
I want to be held.
To be seen in the mess—
and not made into a metaphor.

This body has done
miracles
just by waking up.
This mind has crawled
out of places
no one even noticed I was trapped in.

I don't need your admiration
if it comes with conditions.

What I need
is space.
To stop being a warrior.
To be soft
without being seen as weak.
To be still
without being called lazy.
To be broken
without being discarded.

(Continued on next page)

I don't want perfection.
I want grace.
Raw.
Deserved.
Unapologetic.

Because I am tired
of asking permission
to simply be.

Longing of Acceptance

I am not here
to be manageable.

I've spent too many years
shrinking in mirrors,
swallowing parts of myself
just to make others feel bigger.

I trimmed my truth
into soundbites you could stomach.
Filtered my body
so you wouldn't flinch.
Masked my mind
because you didn't know how to love
a brain like mine.

But I'm done performing
just to be allowed in the room.

You don't get to praise my strength
after making survival my only option.
Don't admire my "resilience"
if you only showed up
for the aftermath
never the war.

I'm obviously different.
And that difference
has never been the problem.
Your discomfort has.

(Continued on next page)

I'm loud when I "shouldn't" be.
Quiet when you expect me to speak.
I stim when I'm anxious.
Shut down when I'm overwhelmed.
I feel in volume.
I live in layers.

And I'm done
apologizing for the shape of me.

My body is not an inconvenience.
My voice is not a malfunction.
My presence is not a disruption.
You don't get to carve me down
to fit your comfort zone.

Because I am not here
to be digestible.
Not here
to be the kind of different
you can swallow without choking.

I'm here to take up space.

All of me.
The too much.
The not enough.
The raw, raging, holy contradiction
I was always meant to be.

So if acceptance means
I have to shrink, perform, or disappear
(Continued on next page)

I'm not asking to be accepted anymore.

I'm accepting myself.
And I will not apologize
for how loud that love sounds
when it finally comes from me.

Longing to Be Chosen

I don't need to be your first choice.
But I want to be a choice.

I want to be chosen
when the light is unforgiving—
when it spills across my skin
and shows every roll on my side,
every scar that stayed,
every wrinkle, every stretch mark,
every blemish
I've tried to make peace with.

I want to be chosen
when I'm not angled just right,
when I'm not dressed to distract,
when my hair is wild
and my laugh is louder than you expected.

Not just at 1 a.m.,
when the world is quiet
and you're lonely enough to remember me.

I want to be thought of
in the middle of your day,
when you're busy,
when you're needed elsewhere,
when there are a hundred easier choices—
and you still pick me.

Choose me

(Continued on next page)

when my body is soft in your hands,
when my skin folds under your touch,
when my face is bare
and you can see every truth
I've ever tried to hide.

I don't need to be your only choice.
But I want to be your real one.
The one you come back to
not because it's easy
but because it's me.

Because I want to know
that you saw it all
and wanted me anyway.

Longing of Love

I want a love
that doesn't vanish
when I stop being easy to hold.

I want a love
that sees the cracks
and chooses me anyway—
not in spite of them,
but because of them.

Not a fantasy.
Not a highlight reel.
Not the kind of love
that only lasts through the good angles
and good moods.

I want the kind
that stays
through silence.
Through shutdowns.
Through the days my body aches
and I don't have the words
to explain why.

I've given love like shelter.
Like oxygen.
I've poured myself into men
who only offered me mirrors—
just enough reflection
to make me stay,

(Continued on next page)

but never enough depth
to make me feel seen.

I've begged in silence.
Smiled through abandonment.
Turned my love into labor,
my body into apology.

But not anymore.

Because I'm not looking
for the kind of love
that asks me to dim.

I want to be kissed
like the world might end—
and held
like I'm the reason it shouldn't.

I want hands
that don't hesitate
when they feel my scars.
A voice that says
I'm still here
when I flinch,
when I freeze,
when I forget I'm worthy of softness.

I don't need perfect.
I don't need promises you can't keep.
I need presence.
Consistency.

(Continued on next page)

Truth.

So no
I'm not desperate for love.
I'm just finally clear
on the kind I deserve.

And if it's not love that sees me
fully,
loudly,
unfiltered

Then I'd rather be alone
with my own damn heartbeat
than ever settle
for someone who only wanted
the pretty version of me.

Because touch fades.
Bodies rest.
But the kind of passion I'm longing for
it stays.
It grows.
It fuels.

Don't just touch me.
Ignite me.
Everywhere.
All at once.
In ways I can't forget.

Longing of Passion

I don't just want safe.
I want passion!
the kind that wakes every part of me
the kind that sets my thoughts alight,
makes my chest tighten,
pulls words out of me
I didn't know I was holding.

I want it to ignite me
not just my skin,
but the place in my ribs
where hope sleeps.
The place in my chest
where joy has been patient.
The corners of my mind
that have gone too quiet.

Feed the fire
that has nothing to do with hands
and everything to do with presence.
Make my pulse race
with a sentence,
with a look,
with the way it make the air feel different
when it walk into the room.

I want passion that lives
in the conversations that haven't finished,
the glances that don't need explaining,
the heat of knowing *(Continued on next page)*

we could stay here all night
and never run out of ways to find each other.

Because touch fades.
Bodies rest.
But the kind of passion I'm longing for
it stays.
It grows.
It fuels.

Don't just touch me.
Ignite me.
Everywhere.
All at once.
In ways I can't forget.

Longing of Desire

Desire is not polite.
It doesn't wait for the right time.
It slips in without warning,
takes up space,
and dares you to try and ignore it.

It's not just my body that remembers
it's my mind.
My thoughts circling back
to the way your voice dips,
the way your words settle into me
like they belong there.

I want the kind of desire
that makes my breath catch
in the middle of an ordinary moment
stirred by a glance,
a sentence,
a silence that hums like a secret.

Desire that isn't just skin-deep
but bone-deep.
Soul-deep.
The kind that feels like hunger and home
at the same time.

It's not about needing you here.
It's about wanting you everywhere.
In the pauses between my sentences,
in the curve of my smile,

(Continued on next page)

in the dreams I wake up from
still tasting your name.

Don't give me a desire that fades.
Give me the kind
that roots itself in me.

That lingers even when the room is empty,
that makes the absence
feel like its own kind of touch.

Because passion is the fire.
But desire
desire is the smoke
that stays in the air long after.

Longing for Intimacy

I don't want to just be undressed.
I want to be bare.

I want you to know
the way my breath changes
when I'm holding back a truth.
The way my laughter tilts
when I'm trying to hide hurt.

I want you close enough
to see the moments
when my guard slips
and not move away.

Because intimacy isn't skin on skin.
It's eye to eye.
It's hearing the break in my voice
and choosing to stay.

It's your hand steady in mine
when my mind is pulling me under.
It's your voice
being the thing that brings me back.

I don't want someone
who only loves the polished version
the filtered, measured, ready-for-the-world me.
I want the one
who will sit with the raw,
the restless.

(Continued on next page)

I want to feel safe enough
to let you see me
in the moments I've spent a lifetime hiding.
And I want to see you there too

no masks,
no performance,
just truth between us.

Because naked fades.
Bare stays.
And I am longing
for the kind of closeness
that can survive the weight
of both.

Epilogue

From the silence, a voice rose—mine.

This journey began with loss.
Not the soft kind,
but the kind that cleaves through your world
and leaves everything echoing.

When my mother passed,
time stilled.
And I was left holding the weight of her absence
with trembling hands.

Grief became my shadow.

For months,
I smiled through the shattering
kept a peaceful home
while a war raged inside me.
I told the world I was okay,
mostly to convince myself.

And when I could no longer carry the quiet alone,
I wrote.

Echoes of Me is what grief, depression, years of silence,
heartbreak, resilience, and longing look like when they're
given a voice.
Every poem, a heartbeat.
Every line, a cry with nowhere else to go.

This book is not closure
it is proof that I'm surviving.

To those walking through their own silence,
this is my hand reaching back.

—L. D. Bailey

Echoes of Me:
A Journey Through Awakening
Preview

Echoes of Me: A Journey Through Awakening
Preview

On my first journey,
somewhere along the way,
in the hollowed space where sorrow once screamed,
I felt something shift.

Something tender.
Something alive.

A remembering.
An awakening.

Desire stirred
not just for touch,
but for self.
For becoming.

If grief cracked me open,
then what comes next
is what dares to grow in the ruins.

A slow awakening.
A sacred unraveling.

First Touch of Wanting.
Unfold Me Slowly.
Earn My Surrender.

The silence taught me how to survive.
Now, I'm learning how to burn.

If you've made it this far,
keep walking with me.

The next echo is waiting.

Her Return

I thought I'd lost her
the woman who burned.

But she wasn't gone.
She was sleeping,
buried under the weight of my exhaustion,
smothered by years of being told
to be smaller,
softer,
quieter.

She waited in the shadows,
watching,
studying the cracks in the walls
I built to survive.
And when the first one split
she stepped through.

Now she's here.
Her fire doesn't just warm
it scorches.
It devours every "should,"
every "less,"
every voice that dares
to tell her she belongs in the dark.

But even flames flicker.
Some days, heat pulls back,
shadows press closer,
and insecurities whisper louder than *(Continued on next page)*

the crackle of her blaze.
I don't always feel beautiful,
I don't always feel powerful.

But her light
even dim
is still mine.

It will never go out.
And I will never again believe
that I don't deserve to feel it.

I Am Not Who I Was

Once, I was a mirror
reflecting everyone else,
shaping myself into the contours of their approval,
polished so smooth
you couldn't see the cracks underneath.

I waited for someone to fill me again
when they walked away,
never realizing
I had always been my own reflection.

Now, I am the glass
and the fire
and the hand that holds them steady.
I do not bend to fit you
you bend to see me.

But even now,
in the glow of my own strength,
there are days I catch my reflection
and doubt stares back.
Days I don't feel beautiful.
Days I forget that desire
is not something I have to earn.

And yet
I carry the truth:
I am not who I was.
Even if I feel small,

(Continued on next page)

I will never shrink back
into the version of me
who didn't know she
deserved to take up space.

Pulse

Something shifted
the first time I stopped holding back.

My laugh was lower,
my gaze lingered longer,
my touch
lingering.

I explored my own skin without apology,
testing the edges of my hunger,
learning what I liked,
letting my body bloom
in the privacy of my own hands.

I didn't need an audience.
I didn't need permission.
This was for me
to see myself as worth craving,
to feel how my own heat moves under my skin.

But there are days
when the pulse softens.
Days when the mirror feels colder,
when I can't find that same spark in my touch,
when beauty feels like a language I can't speak.

Still, the ember stays.
Quiet,
steady,
waiting for breath.

(Continued on next page)

I might not always feel desired
but I will always deserve to be.
And I will always return to myself
until the pulse is loud again.

The Fire Beneath

They think I'm calm.
They think stillness means safe.
They mistake my silence
for absence.

But still water
can drown you faster
than any wave.

I am not cold.
I am waiting.
Holding the match
just out of sight.
Feeling the weight of it in my hand.

Because my fire is not for anyone
who happens to wander close.
It's for the ones who understand
how dangerous it is
to stand this near to me.

I have burned before.
Too fast.
Too bright.
Too easy.
I've lit the wrong hands
and watched them drop me
like something that hurt too much to hold.

(Continued on next page)

So now
I keep it beneath the surface.
In my ribs.
In my spine.
In the places you can't see
until I decide
you've earned the sight of it.

You will think I am still.
But if you pay attention
you'll notice the air shifting.
The heat gathering.
The way your breath catches
without knowing why.

Because the fire is there.
It's always been there.
And when I choose
it will rise.
And you will understand
why I never needed to roar
to be dangerous.

Not for Tears

May I use your shoulders
not to cry,
not to lean,
not to pour out sad little stories...

But to rest my thighs on
while your mouth gets lost between them,
devouring me
like the taste has been haunting you
for years.

I want to feel your breath
spill hot over my skin
right before your tongue
drags slow,
then deep
finding that spot
that makes my grip on you tighten
until my nails dig crescents into your back.

I'm not thinking about heartbreak.
I'm thinking about the way
your jaw flexes
when I grind against your face,
how you growl into me
like you're staking a claim.

You hold me open
like you own the view.

(Continued on next page)

Like you'd fight God
before you'd let me close my legs again
.

And when my thighs tremble?
When I pull at your hair
because I can't take another second
of that rhythm that's wrecking me?

You just grip harder
press me down onto you
make me ride it out
until I'm gasping,
clutching your head,
so far gone
I forget my own name.

That's what your shoulders are for.
Not tears.
Not comfort.

For holding me steady
while I break in the best possible way
over and over
on your tongue.

Tastes Sweet

Whenever I think of you,
I can't help but lick my lips
slow, deliberate,
like my tongue already knows the taste
it's aching for.

I wonder if you'd be sweet
sweeter than honey sliding down my throat,
sweeter than wine clinging to my tongue,
sweeter than sin when it's too good to stop.

Your name rolls off my mouth like nectar,
thick and heavy,
and I want to smear that sound against your skin,
to suck it from your neck
while you groan it back into me.

I imagine your flavor
not just on my lips,
but dripping down my chin,
sticky between my chest,
running down my thighs,
until I'm drenched in you
and the room reeks of sex.

Because I don't just want a kiss.
I want the kind of kiss
that leaves me messy,
that coats my tongue in your hunger,
that stains me so deep

(Continued on next page)

I taste you every time I breathe.

Every thought of you
is a wet ache in my mouth.
Every fantasy is a dripping,
slick promise of what could be.
And my lips?
They're starving.
Starving to know if your heat
is as intoxicating as your name,
if your skin bursts like ripe fruit,
if your body leaks sweetness
I can lap up until my jaw trembles.

Whenever I think of you,
I lick my lips
because imagination isn't enough.
I need your taste
sliding down my throat,
filling me,
wrecking me,
so that I never again
confuse daydream with desire.

I want you dripping
not in metaphor,
but in my mouth,
on my tongue,
soaking every inch of me
until I am nothing but proof
of how sweet you really are.

Deep

How deep do you want to go?
Just skin, just sweat, just the surface tremble
or further,
into the places no one dares to touch?

Deeper than the lips that part in moans,
deeper than the pulse between thighs
I'm talking about hunger,
the kind that rewrites silence
with every stroke,
every gasp,
every prayer made in the dark.

You think depth is only measured in inches.
But depth is the way your voice
slips beneath my ribs,
the way your eyes
push past every wall I built
and break me into confession.

Go deep
not just in me,
but *into* me.
Into the marrow of my fears,
the folds of my memory,
the chaos in my mind
where even I don't wander alone.

(Continued on next page)

Deeper
into the scars I hide under laughter,
the ache I stitch behind my smile.
Touch me there,
with your hands, with your heat,
with your unrelenting desire.

When you thrust,
don't just fuck my body.
Fuck my hesitation.
Fuck the years I thought I was unworthy.
Fuck the ghosts that said
I wasn't enough.

Deeper still—
until my soul arches with my spine,
until my breath leaves as yours enters,
until thought and body collapse
into one relentless fire.

Do you feel it?
This is what deep means—
not just wet, not just tight,
but infinite.
A place where moans turn to prayers,
and prayers turn to screams,
and screams turn to silence—
because words can't live here.

So go deep.
Deeper.

(Continued on next page)

Deeper.
Until you drown in me,
until I drown in you,
until we are nothing but a rhythm
that the universe itself
cannot ignore.

These pages may close,
but the echoes don't end here.

If you felt something in these words,
if you carried even a piece of them with you—
know that my voice continues beyond this book.

For now, you can find me here:
TikTok: @simply.seanie

And soon, there will be more—
a new home for these echoes,
a space still being built,
where silence and story will keep unfolding:
⊕VoicesBeyondSilence.com (coming soon)

Thank you for listening to my echoes,
for carrying them in your own heart.

And always remember:
You are worthy.
You are enough.
You matter.

— L. D. Bailey

www.ingramcontent.com/pod-product-compliance
Lightning Source LLC
Chambersburg PA
CBHW021144090426
42740CB00008B/926